MEET *my* FRIEND

I HAVE A FRIEND

who is always faithful;

who can meet all your needs;

who will never leave you.

This friend is Jesus Christ.

Since I have known him, he has been faithful in all his promises. He is " . . . the same yesterday and today and forever"(Hebrews 13:8). Through my joys and sorrows he has been a "friend who sticks closer than a brother" (Proverbs 18:24).

I first met him when I read his invitation in the Bible: "Come to me, all who labor and are heavy laden, and I will give you rest" (Matthew 11:28). I came to him, and he freed me from my burden of sin and guilt and gave me hope for living.

Daily he meets my needs. He promises, "Peace I leave with you; my peace I give to you. . . . Let not your hearts be troubled, neither let them be afraid" (John 14:27). When I am lonely and worried, I remember his words: "I will not leave you or forsake you" (Joshua 1:5).

I know that even at the hour of death he will remain with me, and one day he will take me to heaven to live with him.

How can you and I be sure of Christ's love? The Bible says, "Greater love has no one than this, that someone lay down his life for his friends" (John 15:13). We can be assured of his love because he, the sinless Son of God, suffered for our sins on the Cross of Calvary.

We can know that Christ's love is everlasting. Because he rose from the grave and returned to the Father in heaven, he can say, "I am the first and the last, and the living one. I died, and behold I am alive forevermore" (Revelation 1:17–18).

Yes, we can trust the Lord Jesus as our eternal friend. He invites us: "Behold, I stand at the door and knock. If anyone hears my voice and opens the door, I will come in to him and eat with him, and he with me" (Revelation 3:20).

If you have never trusted Jesus as your Savior, invite him into your life today. Follow him and he will never fail you. "Truly, truly, I say to you, whoever hears my word and believes him who sent me has eternal life. He does not come into judgment, but has passed from death to life" (John 5:24).

To be enrolled in a free Bible course and to learn more about Christianity, write to Crossway and include your name, age, and address: **Crossway, 1300 Crescent Street, Wheaton, IL 60187**.

If you'd like to talk with someone about Jesus Christ via text or chat, visit **chataboutjesus.com**.

To read the Bible or find a church in your area, visit **Crossway.org/LearnMore**.

www.goodnewstracts.org